ULTIMATE MAC...

Tanks and Military Vehicles

Rob Colson

Published in 2013 by Wayland
Copyright © Wayland 2013

Wayland
338 Euston Road
London NW1 3BH

Wayland Australia
Level 17/207 Kent Street
Sydney NSW 2000

Senior editor: Julia Adams
Produced by Tall Tree Ltd
Editor, Tall Tree: Jon Richards
Designer: Ed Simkins

British Library Cataloguing in Publication Data

Colson, Robert Scott.
  1. Vehicles, Military--Juvenile literature.
  2. Tanks
  (Military science)--Juvenile literature.
  I. Series
  623.7'4-dc23

ISBN: 978 0 7502 8042 6

10 9 8 7 6 5 4 3 2 1

Printed in China

Wayland is a division of Hachette Children's
Books, an Hachette UK company.

www.hachette.co.uk

Picture credits
Cover main istockphoto, cover bl Davric,
cover br US Air Force, 1 US Army, 3 Jason
Merideth/Shutterstock, 4l Slavapolo/Dreamstime.
com, 4-5 US Army, 5t Phillip Capper/GNU,
6 Jmh2o/GNU, 7t Bettmann/Corbis, 7b Ints
Vikmanis/Dreamstime.com, 8 US Army, 9t
Krystyna Wojciechowska Czarnik/Dreamstime.
com, 9b 3 Jason Merideth/Shutterstock, 10
Fiorellino/GNU, 11t Simon Dack Archive/Alamy,
11b US Air Force, 12 US Army, 12-13 US Army,
13t cell105/GNU, 14 US Navy, 15t US Army,
15b US Air Force, 16 US Army, 16-17 Luhai
Wong/Creative Commons Sharealike, 17t US
Army, 18 Davric, 19t US Army, 19b US Army,
20 US Army, 21t US Air Force, 21b US Army,
24 Luhai Wong/Creative Commons Sharealike

Contents

War machines

Motorised vehicles play a major part in warfare. Armoured vehicles carry guns, soldiers or equipment onto the battlefield.

Tanks are heavily armoured, have tracked wheels for travelling over rough areas, and are usually armed with a large gun on a rotating turret. Other armoured vehicles carry troops or help with building work.

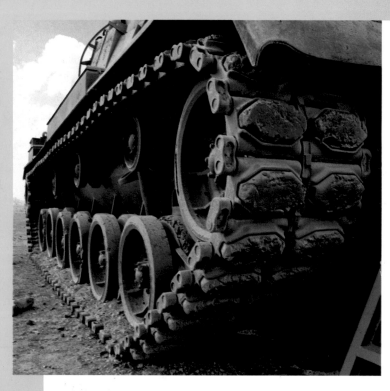

Amazing design

Tanks and many other military vehicles use tracks. This means that a band of linked plates covers the wheels. Tracks spread the weight of the vehicle across a wide area. This stops it from sinking into soft ground.

Early tanks

Tanks were developed during World War I. The British used their first tank, the Mark I, in the Battle of the Somme in 1916. The Mark I was able to cross enemy trenches. It was a great success and more models quickly followed. Germany responded to the new threat by developing special anti-tank guns.

Early tanks such as this British Mark IV from 1917 did not have a main gun on a turret. Instead, guns were fitted to either side of the tank.

A Chinese Type 99 tank fires its main gun. The most advanced tank in the Chinese army, the Type 99 has a powerful 125 mm gun and a top speed of 80 kilometres per hour.

Panzer tanks

The name 'Panzer' comes from the German word for 'armour'. It was the name given to German tanks during World War II.

Germany developed many new Panzers during the war, including the Tiger I, a fearsome tank with strong armour and a powerful gun.

The Tiger I was too heavy to cross small bridges, so it was designed to move through water up to 4 metres deep. This allowed it to cross most rivers.

TECHNICAL DATA

Tiger 1
YEARS OF SERVICE **1942–1945**
ENGINE **Petrol**
NUMBER OF CYLINDERS **12**
ARMOUR **25–120 mm**
MAIN GUN **88 mm**
TOP SPEED **38 kph**
WEIGHT **56.9 tonnes**
CREW **5**
RANGE **195 kilometres**

Big gun

The Tiger I was designed in 1942 to replace the smaller Panzer IV. The Panzer IV did not have a big enough gun to destroy Soviet T-34 tanks, even at close range. The Tiger I was armed with an 88 mm gun that fired huge rounds and could destroy an enemy tank from up to 4 kilometres away. However, it was expensive to produce, and fewer than 1,400 were built. By comparison, the Soviets built 35,000 T-34s.

An American soldier poses on top of an overturned Tiger I in Normandy in 1944. Germany had too few tanks to stop the larger Allied forces.

Amazing design

The Jagdpanzer 38 was a tank destroyer, which is a light tank designed to attack other tanks. It had sloped armour at the front and back. This was designed to deflect enemy shells, causing them to bounce off the armour rather than pierce it.

M4 Sherman

The M4 Sherman tank was built by the United States during World War II, and used by US and British forces.

The Sherman was reliable and easy to maintain, which gave it an advantage over the powerful but less reliable German tanks.

US troops advance through a Belgian town under cover of an M4 Sherman in September 1944. Nearly 50,000 Shermans took part in World War II.

Strength in numbers

The Sherman was a medium-weight tank with thin armour. It had a much less powerful main gun than the German Tiger 1 tank. The front armour of a Tiger was very strong, so the Shermans had to fire on them from the side or the back to damage them. A Tiger could destroy a Sherman from any angle. However, the Shermans won many battles with German tanks by fighting in very large numbers.

The gunner sat on a seat just beneath the turret so that his head was at gun-height.

Amazing design

The Sherman was the first American tank to have a fully rotating gun turret. The turret was fitted with a device called a gyrostabiliser. This kept the gun steady as the tank crossed bumpy ground, allowing the gunner to aim the gun accurately.

TECHNICAL DATA

M4 Sherman
YEARS OF SERVICE
1942–1955
ENGINE **Petrol**
NUMBER OF CYLINDERS **12**
ARMOUR **53 mm at front;
63 mm at side; 40 mm at back**
MAIN GUN **75 mm**
TOP SPEED **48 kph**
WEIGHT **30 tonnes**
CREW **5**
RANGE **193 kilometres**

Challenger 2

The Challenger 2 is a main battle tank built for the British army. Main battle tanks (MBTs) are large tanks that play an important role in modern armies, supporting infantry (soldiers on foot) in battle.

The Challenger 2 is one of the most advanced MBTs in the world. Its powerful main gun has a range of more than 8 kilometres.

A Challenger 2 is protected by a special material called Chobham armour. This is a ceramic that is twice as hard as any metal.

TECHNICAL DATA

Challenger 2
YEARS OF SERVICE **1998–present**
ENGINE **Diesel**
NUMBER OF CYLINDERS **12**
ARMOUR **Chobham armour**
MAIN GUN **120 mm**
TOP SPEED **56 kph**
WEIGHT **62.5 tonnes**
CREW **4**
RANGE **450 kilometres**

Tank crew

The Challenger 2 has a four-man crew. The commander is in charge of the tank. The loader operates the radio, loads the gun and prepares food for the rest of the crew. The driver steers the tank and looks after the engine. The gunner controls the turret and fires the gun. The crew can see outside the tank by looking through periscopes. Each crew member is trained to do all four tasks in case one of them is injured.

The commander of a Challenger tank keeps watch through a periscope. The gunner sits in front of him, controlling the turret.

Amazing design

To find its way around at night, the Challenger 2 is fitted with a night vision sensor in its turret. Night vision either detects heat instead of light or it boosts the small amount of light it detects to create a picture like the one above.

T-72

The T-72 is a Russian main battle tank. It is a very light tank that can cross small bridges that heavier enemy tanks cannot cross.

To keep the tank as small as possible, the crew of the T-72 work in very cramped conditions. There is so little space inside the tank that the crew all have to be no more than 1.6 metres tall.

Amazing design

Many T-72s are fitted with a special type of armour called reactive armour. This is made of special bricks that are fitted to the outside of the tank. The bricks explode when a weapon such as a missile hits them. This explosion destroys the missile before it can get through into the interior of the tank and kill the crew.

An Iraqi T-72 fires its main gun during the Iraq War. Originally made for the Soviet Union and its allies, the T-72 is now used by armies right across the world.

Although it is a small tank, the T-72 is fitted with a very large 125 mm gun. As well as firing at the enemy, the gun barrel can smash through concrete walls up to 40 cm thick.

Laser rangefinder

The T-72's gun is fitted with a laser rangefinder. The rangefinder shines a powerful beam of laser light at the tank's target and measures the time it takes for the beam to be reflected back. The time taken tells the crew how far away the target is.

TECHNICAL DATA

T-72
YEARS OF SERVICE **1973–present**
ENGINE **Diesel**
NUMBER OF CYLINDERS **12**
ARMOUR **Steel and composite**
MAIN GUN **125 mm**
TOP SPEED **48 kph**
WEIGHT **41.5 tonnes**
CREW **3**
RANGE **460 kilometres**

APCs

Armoured personnel carriers (APCs) are designed to carry troops to the battlefield. They are known to soldiers as 'Battle Buses'.

APCs vary widely in design. Some are lightly armoured to protect against small weapons. Others have two layers of heavy armour to protect against powerful explosives. APCs are also fitted with weapons such as machine guns and grenade launchers.

Amazing design

Many APCs are amphibious. This means that they can travel on land and through water. Amphibious APCs are used to carry troops to the shore during an attack from the sea. They are carried close to the shore by special warships called amphibious assault ships.

Ukrainian APCs land on a beach during a training exercise. They power through the water using propellers, just like boats.

Light APC

The M113 (right) is the most widely used APC in the world. It was first developed in the 1960s by the US Army as a vehicle that could be carried into combat zones by plane. Its armour is made from the light metal aluminium. This makes it strong enough to protect its crew from most small weapons fire, but still light enough to be carried by plane.

An M113 finds shelter in a launderette in Panama City during a US operation in Central America. It is small enough to go where larger tanks cannot go.

TECHNICAL DATA

M113

YEARS OF SERVICE **1960–present**
ENGINE **Diesel**
NUMBER OF CYLINDERS **6**
ARMOUR **38 mm aluminium**
MAIN GUN **M2 Browning machine gun**
TOP SPEED **48 kph**
WEIGHT **12.3 tonnes**
CREW **2 plus 11 passengers**
RANGE **480 kilometres**

REV 2A

Engineering vehicles

Military engineering vehicles carry out building work in combat zones. This includes digging trenches or knocking down obstacles.

The vehicles may be diggers, bulldozers, cranes or backhoes – all the vehicles that you find on a building site. They can also be fitted with tools that are only found on the battlefield, such as mine-clearing rakes.

Amazing design

The M728 is an American engineering vehicle. The ones shown above have been fitted with mine-clearing rakes. The rakes lift mines buried in the soil and push them to the side without exploding them. This clears a path wide enough for tanks and other vehicles to follow safely.

Armed engineer

This M728 engineering vehicle is used in demolition (knocking down buildings). It is fitted with a winch for lifting and carrying and a bulldozer blade for pushing over walls. The M728 is also heavily armed, carrying a 165 mm main gun that can be used to blast holes into walls.

The Pionierpanzer Dachs is a German engineering vehicle that is based on the Leopard 1 tank. In place of the main gun, it is fitted with a digging bucket.

TECHNICAL DATA

M728
YEARS OF PRODUCTION
1965–1987
ENGINE **Twin-turbo diesel**
NUMBER OF CYLINDERS **12**
ARMOUR **143 mm**
MAIN GUN **165 mm M135**
TOP SPEED **48 kph**
WEIGHT **50 tonnes**
CREW **4**
RANGE **450 kilometres**
CRANE CAPACITY **8 tonnes**

AVLBs

Armoured vehicle-launched bridges (AVLBs) are combat support vehicles that carry metal bridges.

AVLBs allow tanks and other armoured vehicles to cross rivers. They are needed where there are no other bridges nearby, or where existing bridges are too narrow or too weak to support the weight of heavy armoured vehicles.

Some AVLBs are converted trucks. The chassis (frame) of the trucks needs to be very strong to support the weight of the bridge, which can weigh more than 15 tonnes.

TECHNICAL DATA

M60

YEARS OF SERVICE **1987-present**
ENGINE **diesel**
NUMBER OF CYLINDERS **12**
GEARBOX **2-speed**
RANGE **464 kilometres**
TOP SPEED **48 kph**
CROSS COUNTRY SPEED **12–18 kph**
WEIGHT **51 tonnes**
CREW **2**
BRIDGE LENGTH **19 metres**

Converted tank

The M60 (pictured right) is an AVLB used by the US Army. Its main body is similar to the body of a tank, with tracked wheels to allow it to travel over rough land carrying the bridge on top. The bridge is folded while it is not being used. This kind of folded bridge is called a scissor bridge. When unfolded, the scissor bridge can cover a river that is up to 18 metres wide. It can hold a weight of up to 70 tonnes, strong enough for most kinds of armoured vehicles.

Amazing design

An M60 can make a bridge in less than five minutes. Once the bridge has been unfolded and laid in place, the AVLB detaches itself from the bridge and moves aside to allow the tanks and other vehicles to cross. The AVLB is the last to cross. it reattaches itself to the bridge once it is on the other side, and the bridge is folded back into place.

Robot wars

Some military vehicles are unmanned robots operated by remote control. Robot vehicles are sent to places that are too dangerous or too small to send people.

Robot vehicles have been developed to operate on land, in the air and underwater. Today, most robot vehicles are small and light, but in the future, even large tanks may be unmanned.

TECHNICAL DATA

Ripshaw
YEARS OF PRODUCTION
2009–present
ENGINE SIZE **Diesel**
SUSPENSION TRAVEL **400 mm**
ARMOUR **Unarmed**
TOP SPEED **more than 100 kph**
WEIGHT **4,000 kg**
PAYLOAD CAPACITY **900 kg**
HEIGHT **1.8 metres**

The Ripshaw is an experimental unmanned light tank. It is designed to be fast and flexible. The Ripshaw is not well armoured, but its light frame allows it to accelerate from 0 to 80 kph in just 3.5 seconds.

Amazing design

Unmanned aerial vehicles (UAVs) are used today mostly for reconnaissance missions. This means that they are sent over enemy territory to gather information about enemy positions. In the future, fighter jets will be unmanned. Their human crew will control them safely from the ground using satellite links.

The MQ-1 Predator is a UAV in the US Air Force. It can fly up to 740 kilometres to a target, and remain overhead for 14 hours gathering information before returning to base.

Cameras on this SUGV's head allow its operators to see exactly where it is going.

Small robots

Small unmanned ground vehicles (SUGVs) are light and small enough to be picked up by hand. They are used in military operations in cities, where they can be sent into tunnels, sewers or pipes. SUGVs are controlled using systems originally designed for games consoles.

Glossary

accelerate
To increase in speed.

amphibious
A vehicle is amphibious if it can travel
on both land and water.

armour
A coating of metal or other strong
material that protects tanks from gunfire.

barrel
Part of a gun. The barrel is a long, thin
metal tube through which a bullet is fired.

bulldozer
A machine used in construction to
push large amounts of soil, sand or
rubble from one place to another.

ceramic
A material such as clay that is made very
hard by heating it, then allowing it to cool.

cylinder
A chamber in an engine inside which
pistons pump up and down.

machine gun
A gun that fires many rounds of bullets
very quickly with one pull of the trigger.

occupation
A period during which one country is
ruled by another country that has taken
control by military force. During World
War II, Germany occupied much of Europe.

periscope
A thin tube with mirrors in it that sticks
out at the top of a tank. It allows the
crew to see where they are going.

propeller
A kind of screw at the back of a ship
that rotates to push the ship forwards.
Many amphibious armoured personnel
carriers are fitted with propellers to
power them in water.

range
The distance a vehicle can travel on one
tank of fuel. Also used for the distance
a gun can fire.

reconnaissance
A military mission to find out information
about the enemy. Reconnaissance involves
moving into enemy territory, so it can be
extremely dangerous.

round
A casing that is loaded into a gun. A round
contains gunpowder and a bullet or missile.

turret
A rotating platform on a tank on which the
main gun is mounted.

winch
A machine used to lift heavy objects. A rope
is attached to the object and then wound
around a cylinder to lift the object.

Models at a glance

Model	Years Made	Number Built	Did You Know?
Mark 1	1915–1919	150	While it was being developed, the Mark 1 was called 'tank' to hide its true purpose. The name stuck.
Challenger 2	1993–2002	446	To confuse the enemy, the Challenger 2 can create smoke using smoke grenades fitted to its turret.
M4 Sherman	1941–1943	50,000	The US originally planned to build more than 100,000 M4 Shermans, but they ran out of steel.
Tiger 1	1942–1944	1,347	Today there is just one Tiger 1 left in working order. It is kept running by the Tank Museum in Dorset, England.
T-72	1971–present	115,000	The T-72 was designed to be able to cross small bridges in Eastern Europe that larger tanks could not cross.
M113	First made in 1960	80,000	The M113 is partly amphibious. Its tracks power it through the water.
M728	1965–1987	291	The main gun of the M728 has a short barrel. It fires high explosives during demolition operations.

Websites

www.thetankmuseum.org

The website of the Tank Museum in Bovington, featuring visual tours of the latest exhibitions.

military.discovery.com/videos/top-10-tanks/

Videos of tanks in action, with explanations of their special features.

www.militaryfactory.com/armor/armored-personnel-carriers.asp

Features on armoured vehicles from around the world.

www.iwm.org.uk

The website of the Imperial War Museum in London, with a wealth of information about all aspects of warfare, including the history of tanks and armoured vehicles.

science.howstuffworks.com/military-robot.htm

A guide to the latest unmanned military vehicles, featuring ground vehicles and flying robots. Includes a section on the future of warfare and the technology that will be used on the battlefields of tomorrow.

Index